Getting dressed with PETS

STICKER ACTIVITY BOOK

Om KIDZ
An imprint of Om Books International

It's time for Christmas. The weather is cold and the mood is jolly. And two friends, Aria and Molly, are ready for celebrations.

They wear warm clothes, and decide their pets need warm scarves and caps too. Why don't you help them with your stickers!

Surrounded by toys and their furry pets, Pam and Kelly are having a lovely play date. Paste the stickers and complete the picture of their enjoyable evening.

Sam is out with his pet bunny and
Myra is walking her dog.

But wait, there's a lot missing from the scene. Use your stickers to complete it!

Pg-2
Pg-3
Pg-4
Pg-5

Pg-6

Pg-7

Pg-8

Pg-9

Pg-10

Pg-11

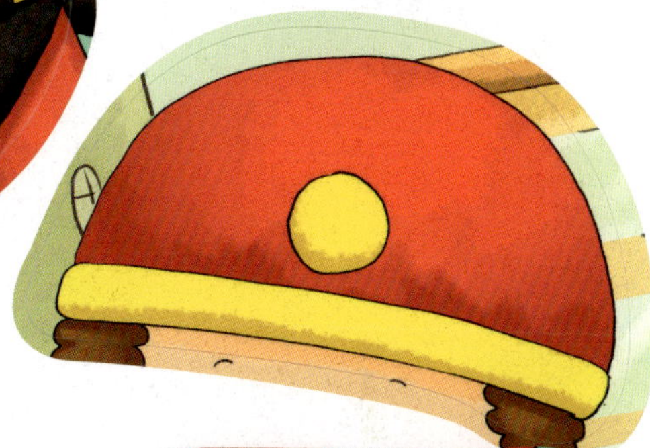

Pg-12

Pg-13

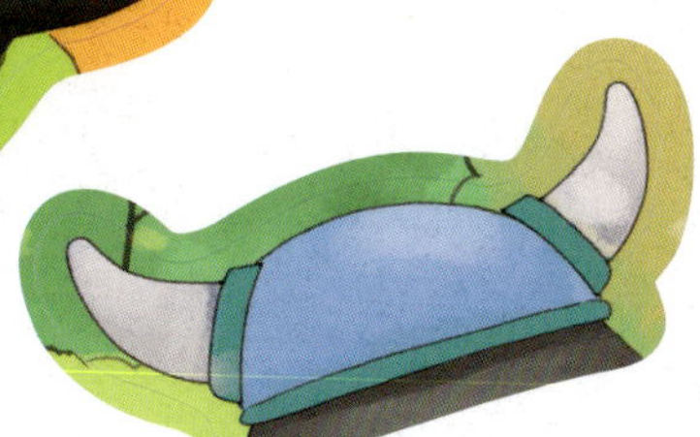

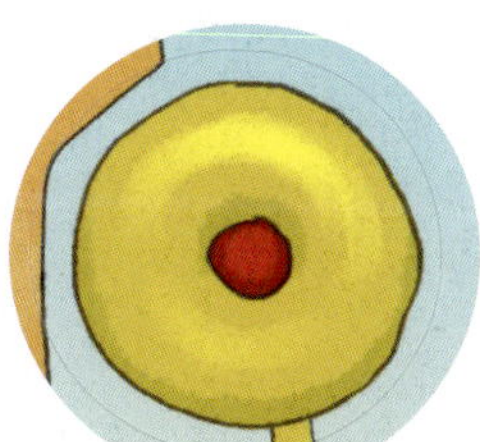
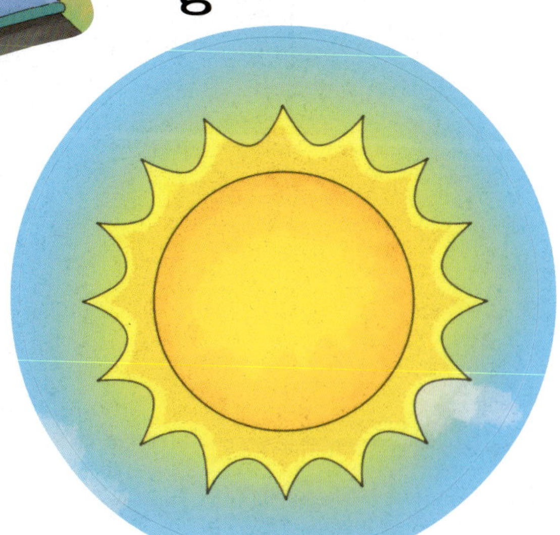

Pg-14

Pg-15

Pg-16

Jill and Lia want to celebrate Halloween. Dress them up with their pets so they can go trick-or-treating and have all the fun!

Superwoman Kate and Superhero Samuel are ready to save the world! And they've got their pets as sidekicks. Dress them up so they are ready to face any challenge!

Help Susan and Andy dress up with their pets for the costume party.

What fun it would be to dress up for Josh's birthday party! Paste the stickers to complete the picture.

HAPPY BIRTHDAY

Molly loves playing with her pets. Join them in their fun by pasting the stickers!